An Eye For An Eye For An Eye | Ellen Renton

Published in 2021 by Stewed Rhubarb
9 Anderson Terrace, Tarland
Aberdeenshire, AB34 4YH

www.stewedrhubarb.org

© Ellen Renton 2021

The moral right of Ellen Renton to be
identified as author of this work has been asserted.

Printed & Bound by Imprint Digital, UK

ISBN: 978-1-910416-18-1

'Contact' was first published in UEA postgraduate anthology: *poetry* 2018; 'On Leaving Early' in *Magma* 77 (as 'Young For My Age'); and 'in my best dreams' in *Pushing Out the Boat* 16. 'What Athena Saw When Tiresias Looked' was originally written for a film by the same name directed by Douglas Tyrrell Bunge, and created with support from Unlimited, Creative Scotland, and Glasgow Tramway.

How Far Can You See? ✳ *5*

Contact ✳ *6*

All The Choirs ✳ *8*

Still ✳ *10*

On Arriving Early ✳ *12*

Junkit ✳ *13*

Cycle ✳ *14*

Good Girl ✳ *15*

How Far Can You See?? ✳ *16*

What Athena Saw When Tiresias Looked ✳ *17*

New Prescription ✳ *21*

Boomerang ✳ *22*

On Leaving Early ✳ *24*

Dermatology ✳ *25*

in my best dreams ✳ *26*

How Far Can You See??? ✳ *27*

Inventory/Prayer ✳ *28*

Cured ✳ *30*

Manifesto For A Perfect Day ✳ *31*

How Far Can You See?

My glasses are fitted for a 6 48 prescription. So, one eighth. Twelve and a half percent of vision. If you stood forty eight metres away from something, picture that, I would need to stand six metres away to have the same view. Imagine a tower no that's a bad imagine a face no imagine a plant yes a plant in a pot imagine it. Now imagine what it looks like when you stand forty eight metres away from it. That's how I would see the same plant in a pot from six metres away. But only on days without glare or weak sun or low sun or hot sun or snow or weather. And only in rooms without strip light or blue light or dimmed light or strobe light or skylights and only when I am slept and watered and only when the ground is even like an iced corner of cake and only when I have fewer than seven worries and upwards of ten minutes and only when I know the plant and I chose the pot and it speaks my name in a voice that sounds like melting and only when I am calm enough and quiet enough and free enough to hear it.

Contact

drawn folds show blotched dawn
yawn
roll on robes of smoke
thoughts fog-soaked   raw
       hold on
crawl to Os of hope
to know more   compose
       don't drop
those globes won't thaw
what floats throatlocked
all floor-torn
                 oh
     not on nose
own goal
     slow
     not launched nor thrown
       so close
    soft   go on

left – done
one down one to go
please lend me the world whole
not kept under dust for someone else
      ugh, nearly
too early
to beg for body to work yet   each bone
sleep poached
      forget the rush, don't
      leap or rub just
      gentle touch
            yassssss

each time I'm almost surprised
by what the morning looks like but
not quite
today it woke me speechless
 now I've got my tongue back

All The Choirs

As the nurse washed
the blood out she said
*angel hair, so you
have, angel hair*

Once when I was wee I thought
I had the stigmata

Anna sang Panis Angelicus
at school mass and we knew
she was brilliant but couldn't
cry like the parents

My brother had a cap signed
by his favourite   after
the EPO it was still there
but less looked-at

In the Angel Gabriel song
we would change the words to *most
highly flavoured lady*   I imagined
that Mary's flavour was
salt and vinegar because
she was always wearing blue

Someone asked the journalist
how we could start fixing things
and he said *we really must stop
believing in angels*

The first time
I played the villain in panto
I wished the booing audience
would register my nuance

I can't picture an angel
afraid to tread

We studied empire like it was a half
remembered gap year and wars like
we were prefects rounding up bullies
at breaktime

Once I thought I saw
a burning bush but maybe
it was a still-lit cigarette's carnage

When we heard the news
we thought we might know
the girl and never thought we
might know the boy accused

*Still**

as in   empty inbox   every morning

that isn't split by my

shoes   as in   the most delicious

hours are underage

contraband stash poured down the drain

and I hold my face

like I didn't want a drink anyway

   the usual dream

in which I drive   only to slap myself

awake when I crash

in the motorway's upset gut   as in

sitting by the window

for the body I was promised   waiting

to be let down again

like a girl in a song   a doubting Thomas

with his knuckles deep

in my roots as if that's where I keep

the answers   as in

that street I shushed by walking

down it   the lips

of the whole top deck but hers – *mate*

have you ever seen

someone so fuckin ugly   as in   a wee life

under engine threat

   feet forgetting their only job and hands

clapping the silver

bonnet   a tableau but for family screams

*As in, 'do you still have a lifelong condition?'

On Arriving Early

I know Glasgow by its toilets I have wasted
time in   all the lids that taught my back
the inhumanity of plastic   did and
undid myself   watched a phone clock
jog on   counted the seconds between
each burp of the boiler   like it were real
thunder   knowing a plaything lock
wouldn't save me from it   undid   did
long division and checked if my last meal
could be guessed from my gums   un
did   wondered who knew the girl
undoing herself a few cubicles down
    would we leave at the same time to dance
a thicklimbed Charleston at the hand dryer
    beg each other to go first

Junkit

after seeing someone painted to look like me in a film

it was the greatest challenge of my career but it was a privilege
i had to teach my body to forget all of what it takes for granted
it's incredible what they can do with prosthetics these days
i had six hours in the make up chair every day for my sins
i suppose it's not just about disability, it's a metaphor
i took my body to extremes of physicality every day
i had to do it justice but it took its toll on my body
i suppose good stories are what makes us human
and i was determined to do this story justice
it's a metaphor and it's not just physicality
i had to teach myself what they can do
i had six hours in make up for my sins
i had to forget all of what my body is
it was a challenge but it's incredible
i think this story makes us grateful
but i try to ignore the Oscar hype
it's incredible what they can do
it took its toll on my metaphor
i was determined to forget me
i suppose it's about disability
it was the greatest challenge
i had six hours in make up
i try to do my body justice
i had to forget incredible
it's not about extremes
i suppose it's a sin
it's a good story
it's a privilege
i try to forget

Cycle

Once a month my stomach bloats
and on the least likely day
I play pregnant   wear something
shapeless over the bump

When we realised what our bodies were
capable of someone said   *no one knew
her mum was pregnant from
behind   wouldn't that be ideal?*

I drank coffee in a place I used to live
and every child that screamed was called
Ethan   I had never noticed
that all who unravel under their coats
bargain with a boy of the same name

There are so many people on TV
who let each other down and I wonder
how babies keep on being born,
why isn't everyone scared
to love something that much

Good Girl

after Alejandra Márquez Abella

I want to wear red silk like
la señora does, keep my head
at home in a magazine while my
self goes to lunch. I know I couldn't
smoke because I've been told
the act doesn't suit my hands
but I could plan a birthday
beyond my means – oh to worry
about the colours of spilled drinks.
If the worst crime I could be
accused of was hiding a life
in my jewellery box then I would
train my face to slip from sunshine
to set cement. It's not often
that I covet her fate but tonight
I'd like to wrap an already-given
gift and take it to a party that
claims it doesn't want me.
I would swim into the room
and make the walls my mirrors.

How Far Can You See??

I find your shape
in thick falling fog;
eyesnoselips
hasty errors
crumbed in grey
from rubbings out.
Do you pull morning
tight around yourself
like a coat
or does it wear you?
From here
you are barely line
and the only thing
that your legs look like
is one of my early works –
a page greased
with crayon
that frowning teachers
tossed aside.

What Athena Saw When Tiresias Looked

One – Athena

She wanted guilt,
for once. In girlhood
she had forged apologies
for the audacity
of a bare ankle
and the carve of her hips,
for the pure cheek
of her height and breath
but she'd never tried
deliberate crime.
A long week
lent the water its tint –
was bathing
brazen?
He watched her
like she was his
inheritance
and when she stole
the colour from his eyes
she nearly smiled.
The boys would still sit
chatting sin.
She couldn't buy
the confidence
of a saunter in darkness

but she could
stop him.
He begged her
bring the colours back
but she tested guilt
in her hands
and liked its weight,
a sore and
honest thing.

Two – Tiresias

He learned
how to live
without edges,
no clue where he
ended and the sky
began.
He used to shout
over sounds
that now gave an outline
when his memory
sketched
the look of the last time
an eye for
an eye
for an eye.
His guilt was the sort
to change its mind,
chalk clouds
in his thoughts then
slink off
but he knew,
that day he leapt
over the line
between taking and
stealing a look.
Now he measured
the ground ahead
in decades
and with his other sight
he watched the blind

shred his name
like paper,
as the future
built an empire
on the back of his tale
and sold the sightless
like a gift shop wonder,
as their voices
were demanded to sail
when others
couldn't make their words
tread water,
as shame and magic
were written into them
forever.

New Prescription

The day is Sunday / lap of honour
for the dying August / a late
entry to the charts / denim jackets /
last scrap of blue fought over like
it's the final slice of something
gorgeous /
      The park is all talk /
all promenade / all bike wheel wink /
*we could be anywhere in the world
eh* / sky open like a map / a
carnival crowd to announce
each ripple on the duck pond / more
bodies than path /
      The tree is a
proper marvel / where the wee road
meets the big road / as it always
has been / but somehow holy /
an old friend whose new haircut
reminds you / you stopped
watching their face long ago

Boomerang

I never used to get
cold boobs in the bath
but now they're in the way

of the water   I feel
like I am in a book
written by a man   I am

a neighbour or detective
who follows her femininity
through doors but

is actually clever too.
Without my glasses
the bath looks twice

its length   The taps might
as well be Inchcolm
and Inchgarvie lost under haar

but my toes have reached
the other enamel shore
and my back sits on a tilted

axis to let my legs
submerge   I can't imagine
the physics of two people

fitting like we did
as children.
Those baths were infinite

when hygiene was soap's
least noteworthy purpose
and no one needed

a moment   but now
I need a sea to keep
all of me covered.

On Leaving Early

At another party I am tripped up
by a tune that sounded familiar but grew
into something else   the words
I am singing do not fit in the spaces
between drums   but the dancer
beside me has the beat in his knees –
across the room so does she   each dancer
is two people   I notice in the half light
how their limbs are in sync like
everyone rehearsed this   slick-rhythmed
bop shimmy kick that I will never have
the legs or hips for   are they all
taking lessons while I make lists and wait
for buses?   my days are all middle now
and night is a rolling deadline   there is no
edge by which my movements can hang
in shadow on the wall   there is no chorus
to the song   or if there is the music never
reaches it   the dancers would not call this
waiting   they are happy to close their eyes
and follow   so there is no one
to see me stop   hunt down my coat

Dermatology

back here again thinking
about that drug I took
for acne   cup to pee in
passed over   *just in case,
this stuff could kill a baby* –
bit much   skipped last period
to be there and god thought
what a hoot   had no miracles
planned but still he watched
the colour get worried
off the waiting room walls
   woman at the desk says
she remembers me   desperate
fib   how come because I don't
know the girl who sold summer
for a smooth forehead   I am
much too cruel and clear-skinned
to thank her now   today's test
is different, I profile a mole –
yes it hurts and no blood
but a new red but rough but
raised   god's thinking aw
bless her   ten years and still
that same nails-in-the-hairline
when she's afraid   same awful
noise from the corner telly

in my best dreams:

the weather doesn't warrant my smart coat but I wear it   we steam to the peak of the only hill in Norfolk and running is a freedom, not an ugly rush   you are full of ice cream and your own jokes   high branches catch ribbons of your rarest laugh, the one that starts in your shoes and rattles your cheekbones like the bars of a cell   you tell me to read poetry in place of mediocre minds and I marvel at your answers to what I haven't asked yet   there are no trains to catch   we make a game of renaming colours   of wishing well on the boys that blew their chances   of finding each other's face in the shapes of the countryside   I mention the rumours of rain   the sky doesn't flinch

How Far Can You See???

Imagine you ask someone for help.
They say, do you like my new coat?
You say yes and ask for help.
They say, I bought it only yesterday.
You say it's lovely and ask for help.
They say, you are so brave and persistent.
You say thank you and ask for help.
They say, what do you think of this cosy lining?
You ask for help.
They say, I admire you, so brave and so persistent.

Inventory/Prayer

bless a beautiful song that wrestles hold music
to the carpet

        bless an expert set of steps
and the punctured lung of a loyal bus

                                bless
yellow

        bless the sky when it reads my mind
and bless the things I learn about the film
after watching it

        bless a friend who unmasks
my panic like it were a budget baddie and not
a real monster

        bless comic sans and all other
things clean

        bless a friend whose laugh looks
like runaway fruit

        bless a sacred lightbulb
bless a borrowed top

        bless factor fifty
with the only sleazy grip I'll forgive

            bless that
wee pocket inside the big pocket

            bless
a friend with April's patience

            bless a friend
who holds me by the shoulders like I am
the perfect dress

Cured

Granny's new hearing aids have retuned
the earth. The wind starts inside her now.
Grandad stacks the dishes jungle loud
while she begs the telly watch its tone.

In the dream where a doctor's hands
become God's own and they fix me up
good and proper, I worry about the angles
in my thanks – *of course I'm grateful* but

how could I stomach the whole world
at once? Have you ever seen a seagull
bloat to spitfire overnight? It might be nice
to fear a falling leaf instead of early death

but how could I live with such colossal
raindrops? *I appreciate your alchemy*
and the new depth in a face but I can't
hack all these colours I've no name for

and how would there be time to swallow
everything subtitled and would I
barter with my eyes to get them closed
like a mother digging into her reserves?

Manifesto For A Perfect Day

I'll step into a morning like a pre-planned outfit.
Everything will be folded, streets will tuck in sharp

corners   No neck will slip sideways
when I am spoken to and eyebrows won't

hit the roof   I will write things into
existence – you will trust my language

so you won't frame my eyes as fidgets.
My knees won't read like a miserable history

and I'll have forgotten what it was to fall
for anything   I will be the butt of no one's joke

not a lazy script not a bitter mouth not a split
pavement   I will enjoy the surprise party

when heat thinks to give weather forecasts
the slip   No one will sell a month's daylight

for a bus pass or a blue badge and I will
gladly stand at the back of a queue with no

need for the extra time   I won't skip
any sleep to explain myself or pay

the premium for a clear metre   I will walk
a quiet way home   Someone will stop

to comment on the colour of my shoes.

Ellen Renton is a poet, performer, and theatre maker from Edinburgh. Her writing has been published in *Gutter, Magma,* and *Pushing Out The Boat*, and she has performed at venues and festivals around the UK. She is a co-founder of In The Works spoken word theatre company and the creator of *Within Sight,* a one-woman poetry show about albinism, ableism, and the Paralympics. In 2020 she collaborated with Scottish electronic musician Lord of the Isles on a climate-themed EP, released by London label AD 93. Find more at *ellenrenton.co.uk*

An audio recording of these poems is available on Soundcloud:

shorturl.at/fEKN6

STEWED RHUBARB